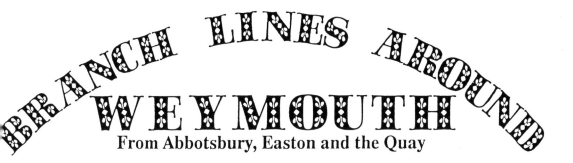

BRANCH LINES AROUND WEYMOUTH

From Abbotsbury, Easton and the Quay

Vic Mitchell and Keith Smith

Published to mark the centenary of
the opening of the Weymouth Quay
Tramway to passenger traffic.

*Cover picture details are
given in caption no. 63.*

Design - Deborah Goodridge

First published July 1989

ISBN 0 906520 65 7

Copyright - Middleton Press, 1989

Typeset by Barbara Mitchell

*Published by Middleton Press
Easebourne Lane
Midhurst, West Sussex
GU29 9AZ
Tel. (0730) 813169*

*Printed & bound by Biddles Ltd,
Guildford and Kings Lynn*

CONTENTS

ACKNOWLEDGEMENTS

We are very grateful for the information and help received from so many of those mentioned in the photograph credits.   As with previous publications we are most appreciative of the assistance given to us by G. Croughton, N. Langridge, E. Staff, N. Stanyon and our ever supportive wives.

INDEX

Diagram of the routes included in this album.

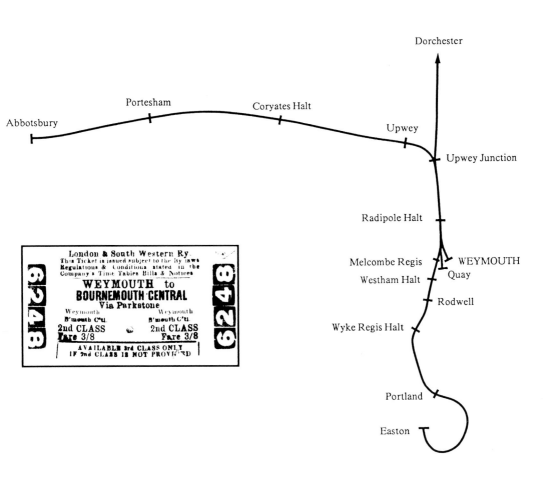

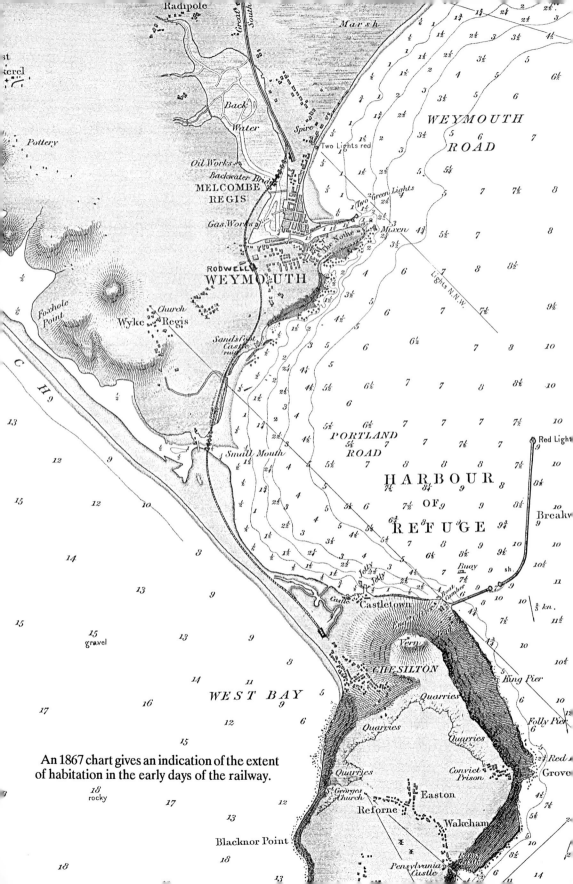

An 1867 chart gives an indication of the extent of habitation in the early days of the railway.

GEOGRAPHICAL SETTING

The east-west ridge of Chalk across South Dorset makes the northern boundary of the area covered by this album. The Abbotsbury branch ran at the foot of the Chalk, the villages it served having developed on the spring line.

The main line to Weymouth runs roughly parallel to the short River Wey, which arises near Upwey and runs south into Radipole Lake. This flows into the Backwater, which bisects the urban area of Weymouth and drains into Weymouth Bay at the harbour. The relatively level land north of Weymouth is based mainly on London Clay.

South of the town, Wyke Regis rises to nearly 200ft on a bed of Limestone which extends east to The Nothe, a headland south of Weymouth Harbour.

Until a road bridge was built, the only direct connection between the mainland and the Isle of Portland was the nine-mile long bank of pebbles known as Chesil Beach.

The Easton branch ran along the southern part of this unusual structure to reach Portland, which is not a town but comprises a number of villages, a prison, a Naval Depot and numerous stone quarries. The main communities are at Fortuneswell, in the north, and at Easton, near the centre. The limestone mass of Portland rises to nearly 500ft above sea level and has yielded vast quantities of high quality, durable building stone for use in the cities of this country and abroad. The railway rose from sea level to 280ft at Easton by means of a circuitous route, largely close to the sheer cliffs of the east coast.

The maps are to scale of 25" to 1 mile, unless otherwise stated.

HISTORICAL BACKGROUND

The Great Western Railway's broad gauge line to Weymouth was opened on 20th January 1857 and was fitted with a third rail south of Dorchester to accommodate the standard gauge trains of the London & South Western Railway. Thus from the outset, passengers could arrive in London at Paddington or Waterloo.

In 1862, the Weymouth & Portland Railway Act was passed, authorising construction of dual gauge lines to Portland and to Weymouth Quay. The former was operated jointly by the GWR and the LSWR, the latter being worked for freight only by the GWR, with horses provided locally. The lines were both brought into use on 16th October 1865.

All broad gauge working had ceased by 18th June 1874 and in 1880 steam locomotives were introduced on the Quay Tramway, all traffic being handled by the GWR. In 1875, a branch was laid onto Admiralty property at Portland and was mainly used for carrying coal to the ships. It was completed in 1876 and opened in 1878.

The six mile long branch from Upwey Junction to Abbotsbury was opened for passengers and freight on 9th November 1885.

Four years later, the Quay Tramway was extended to the pier and passenger trains began to run to and from the Channel Islands ferries on 4th August 1889.

In 1867, a new company started to build a railway south from Easton to convey stone via an incline to a pier at Church Hope Cove. The line was not completed, it later being extended north to Portland via part of the Admiralty's breakwater line. Freight services commenced on 1st October 1900 and passengers were first carried on 1st September 1902. The original terminus at Portland was closed to passengers on 7th May 1905.

Following the formation of the Southern Railway in 1923, the GWR ceased to work the Portland branch but continued to operate the Quay Tramway.

One of the effects of nationalisation in 1948 was the rationalisation of management which resulted in the transfer of all lines south of Dorchester to the Southern Region.

1952 brought the withdrawal of passenger trains from the Easton line on 2nd March and, on 1st December, total closure of the Abbotsbury branch, except for freight facilities at Upwey, which remained until 1962. Goods services ceased on the route to Easton on 5th April 1965 and at Weymouth on 14th August 1972.

Major changes in main-line traction took place on 9th July 1967, when steam was eliminated, and on 16th May 1988, when electric services commenced.

PASSENGER SERVICES

The frequency of trains per day for selected years is shown in the following tables. Column 1 indicates the typical weekday service, column 2 shows the additional trains on Saturdays, while column 3 gives the Sunday frequency.

PORTLAND

	1.	2.	3.
1869	8	-	5
1890	9	-	5
1906	14	-	7
1914	23	1	7
1925	19	2	9
1934	20	-	12
1944	12	-	7
1952	18	-	8

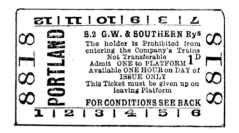

Almost all trains terminated at Weymouth (or Melcombe Regis after 1909). The 1934 timetable shows an exception - the first up train on Sundays ran to Portsmouth and the last down service originated from there.

EASTON

The table shows those Portland services that were extended to Easton.

	1.	2.	3.
1906	4	-	-
1914	4	-	-
1925	6	1	-
1934	6	2	3
1944	3	-	-
1952	6	-	-

ABBOTSBURY

Most trains were shown to terminate at Weymouth, although in some cases the stock worked through to Portland.

	1.	2.	3.
1890	4	-	-
1906	7	-	2
1914	5	-	-
1925	5	2	-
1934	8	-	4
1944	5	-	-
1952	6	1	-

WEYMOUTH QUAY

Passenger trains were operated solely in connection with the mail steamers, thus there was one journey daily from London from 1889, connecting with the night boat. The availability of an additional platform from May 1933 resulted in the introduction of a regular boat train from Birmingham. (The new berth was officially opened on 13th July 1933).

Regular services were suspended during World War II but in the 1950s holiday traffic increased enormously. Up to five boat trains were required on Saturday afternoons in the summer of 1961, following the cessation of sailings from Southampton. For a short while two or three trains were also required to connect with the night sailings.

The decline started in the 1960s and trains for night boats seldom ran after November 1962. Although a DMU service to Bristol was provided in the summers of 1983 and 84, traffic continued to decline and the remaining summer service to Waterloo ceased on 26th September 1987.

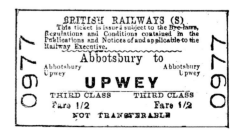

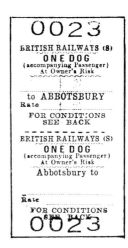

SOUTHERN & GREAT WESTERN RAILWAYS.

WEEKLY SEASON TICKET.   **FIRST CLASS**

No. 140

17
Rate 18s. 6d.

Available between Stations shewn on back hereof

From   To

This Ticket is issued and accepted subject to the Bye-laws, Regulations and Conditions published in the Companies Time Tables, Bills & Notices. It must be produced or delivered up on demand (or the ordinary fare paid) and surrendered immediately on expiry or forfeiture. Any unlawful use of this ticket by any person or persons whomsoever may render such person liable to prosecution. It is **NOT TRANSFERABLE** and remains the property of the issuing Company. This ticket is not valid unless signed.) BY ORDER.

Signature of Holder

0023

BRITISH RAILWAYS (S)
ONE DOG
(accompanying Passenger)
At Owner's Risk

to ABBOTSBURY
Rate
FOR CONDITIONS
SEE BACK

BRITISH RAILWAYS (S)
ONE DOG
(accompanying Passenger)
At Owner's Risk

Abbotsbury to

Rate
FOR CONDITIONS
SEE BACK
0023

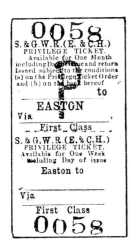

0058
S. & G.W.R. (E. & C.H.)
PRIVILEGE TICKET.
Available for One Month
including Day of Issue and return
Issued subject to the conditions
(a) on the Privilege Ticket Order
and (b) on the back hereof

to

EASTON
Via

First Class

S. & G.W.R. (E. & C.H.)
PRIVILEGE TICKET.
Available for One Week
including Day of issue
Easton to

Via

First Class
0058

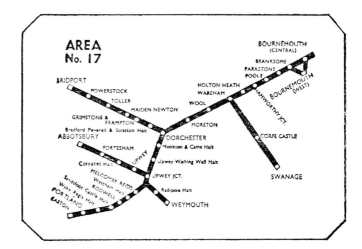

AREA No. 17

September 1925

WEYMOUTH and ABBOTSBURY (Motor Cars—One class only).—Great Western.

	Down.	Week Days only.		Up.	Week Days only.

MELCOMBE REGIS (WEYMOUTH), PORTLAND, and EASTON.—Southern and Great Western.

A Melcombe Regis (Weymouth).   B or ẞ Weds. and Sats.   E or Ɛ Mons. to Fris.   H Through Train from Portsmouth,
J Through Train to Portsmouth.   S or Ş Saturdays.

August 1934

1. Easton Branch   EASTON

1. The line from a new station at Portland was opened to passengers on 1st September 1902, freight having been carried since 1st October 1900. This is the northward view, shortly before the opening.
(Weymouth and Portland Museum)

2. Looking north, soon after the station was burnt out on 28th November 1903, we see the goods line passing under what was then known as Reforne Street. The line led to two loops, each of which held eight wagons and were known as Sheepcroft Siding. A 2.5 ton capacity crane was provided there, for loading stone.
(Lens of Sutton)

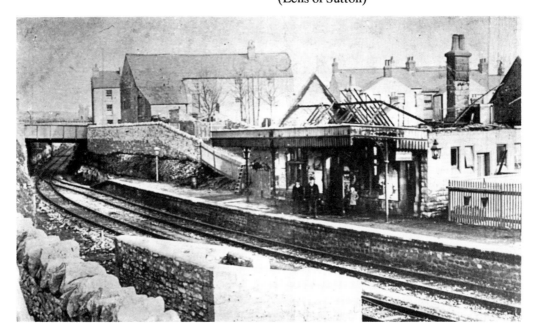

3. The station roof was restored to its original profile but a smaller lamp was provided. The 6 ton goods crane is visible beyond the up starting signal. On the left is the engine shed which came into use on 6th February 1905. (Lens of Sutton)

The 1902 edition shows the close proximity of the station to the town centre and to the Park Quarries. The line north of the station was for goods traffic only.

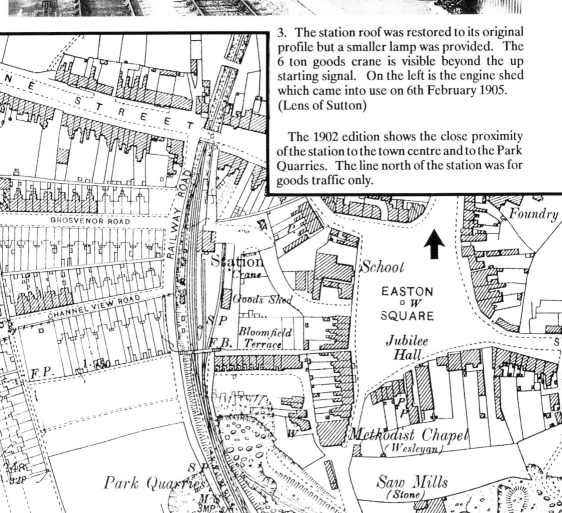

4. Repainting was in progress as class O2 no. 177 waits to depart on 28th May 1929. For many years, the amount spent on station maintenance was in proportion to the receipts. (H. C. Casserley)

5. Another well groomed O2 basks in the afternoon sun at the most southerly outpost of the Southern, excepting Plymouth. The signalmen had special instructions to prevent vehicles running down the steep gradient (1 in 40) southwards. (Lens of Sutton)

The 1902 survey, reduced to 5" to 1 mile, has the southern part of the Portland Railway connecting with the quarry lines, top left. Top right is the Easton & Church Hope Railway from Portland, its circular course to Easton being evident.

6. Class O2 0-4-4T no. 233 runs past the rose-clad signal box to run round its train on 29th August 1938. The coaches in this and the previous two photographs were ex-railmotor vehicles. (J. R. W. Kirkby)

7. Looking south, we can see through the engine shed and note the wagon probably waiting to be loaded with the heaps of locomotive ash. The guard, with shunting pole underarm, approaches the driver standing by the pigeon basket. Maybe class O2 no. 193 was about to visit Sheepcroft sidings. (Lens of Sutton)

8. For some years, a selection of impressive fossils from local quarries was displayed on the platform. The goods shed roof is in the background. Wartime restrictions led to the withdrawal of passenger services to Easton from 1941 to 1944, except during the summer months. (E. H. Seward/J. H. Lucking coll.)

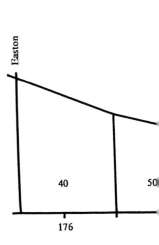

Easton

40   50

176

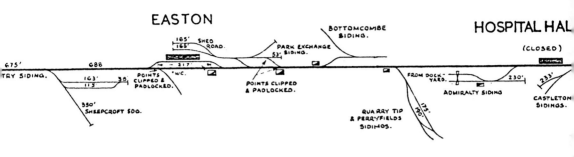

EASTON

BOTTOMCOMBE SIDING.

HOSPITAL HAL

(CLOSED)

165' SHED ROAD.
165'

PARK EXCHANGE SIDING.
53'

675'

688

TRY SIDING.

163'
115
38

POINTS CLIPPED & PADLOCKED.

'WC.

POINTS CLIPPED & PADLOCKED.

FROM DOCK YARD.

230'

233'

ADMIRALTY SIDING

CASTLETON SIDINGS.

350'
SHEEPCROFT SDG.

QUARRY TIP & PERRYFIELDS SIDINGS.

175'

The WWII control diagram showed the position of the various private sidings for stone traffic.

9. Features of interest are the multi-pulleyed GWR-style loading gauge, the goods dock (right) and the provision of catch points in both tracks to arrest runaways. The numerous passengers had come on 1st March 1952, to witness the last day of operation. Class O2 no. 30179 is heading the 5.19pm, which was composed of four Western Region coaches. The signal box remained in use until 24th April 1955. (J. J. Smith)

10. Several enthusiast's specials visited the line after withdrawal of passenger services. This is the RCTS tour on 14th August 1960. The footbridge carried a public footpath and was not intended for passengers. (P. Hay)

Lower right

11. Swindon-built 0-6-0PT no. 4689 looks at home alongside the GWR style water tank in 1962. The building survived for many years, devoid of its canopy. The site is now occupied by Ladymead Hall, a residence for elderly people. (C. L. Caddy coll.)

13. A serious landslip occurred in November 1907, extensively displacing the track. In 1928, a wire screen, over 200yds long, was installed to interrupt and detect rockfalls. It was connected to signals which were automatically set to danger in the event of an obstruction. (C. L. Caddy coll.)

12. Class O2s no. 30177 and 30197 worked the 1.53pm departure from Easton on 1st March 1952, a sad and memorable day for many. On the right is Park siding, used for loading dressed Portland stone. (D. Cullum)

14. An Easton bound train snakes round the curves below the buildings of H.M.Prison. The severe curvature necessitated a ban on the use of six-wheeled coaches and vans. The gradient restricted down coal trains to *nine* wagons and two manned brake vans were required! (Lens of Sutton)

15. A 25mph speed limit was in force south of Portland and, in addition to natural hazards, drivers were required to keep a look out for red flags on the Admiralty Rifle Range. Class O2 no. 213 heads an up train in about 1935, the ex-railmotor coaches displaying their unusual ventilating windows. (Dr. I. C. Allen)

16. The bedding planes of the famous Portland building stone are obvious as nos. 30179 and 30197 pass under the bridge carrying the footpath to Church Hope Cove. The train is the 3.17pm from Easton on the last day of public traffic, 1st March 1952. (D. Cullum)

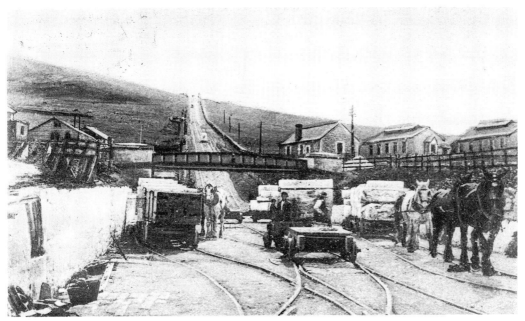

17. The Portland Railway was also known as the Merchant's Railway or Freeman's Incline and was in use from 1826 until 1939. Always gravity and horse worked, it had the unusual gauge of 4' 6" and carried stone exclusively. On the right is part of the Royal Naval Sick Quarters, the bridge being for the Portland-Easton line. (Weymouth Local History Museum)

The 1903 map, reproduced at 5" to 1 mile, gives the relationship of the Admiralty Breakwater and Depot (right) to the original Portland station (lower left). Its successor is not shown, as it was not completed until 1905. Left of centre is the incline of the 4' 6" Portland Railway.

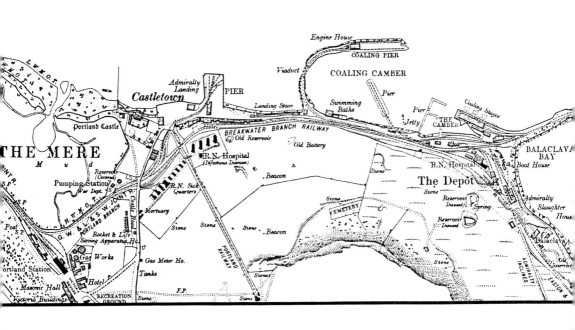

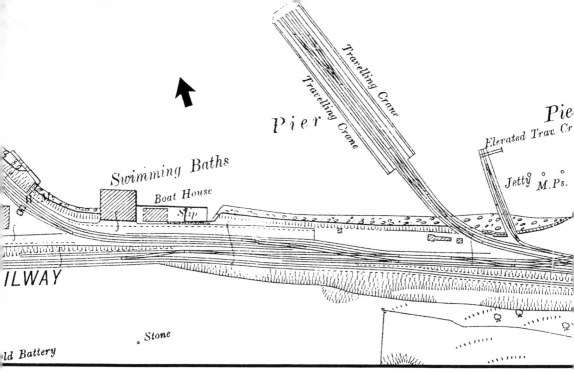

In the map: Travelling Crane · Travelling Crane · Pier · Elevated Trav. Cr · Pie · Swimming Baths · Boat House · Slip · Jetty M.Ps. · ILWAY · Stone · ld Battery

18. Stone quarrying generates large volumes of waste material and steam haulage of this to the tips was practised from an early date. The 0-4-2T locomotive is *Excelsior* , built by W. Bagnall in 1888 and formerly used on the Kerry Tramway. (E. H. Seward)

19. Twelve coach trains for Navy personnel could enter the dockyard but in the 1960s they had to be double headed with 57XX class 0-6-0Ts as far as Portland goods yard, where one engine would be put on the rear of the train.   On reaching the Admiralty lines, the leading engine would be detached and the one at the rear would then propel the train into the yard.   This photograph shows a less complicated movement within the yard on Navy Day in 1961, the locomotive being Andrew Barclay no. 1570 of 1917.   It was the last steam locomotive in the dockyard and was scrapped in 1963. (C. L. Caddy)

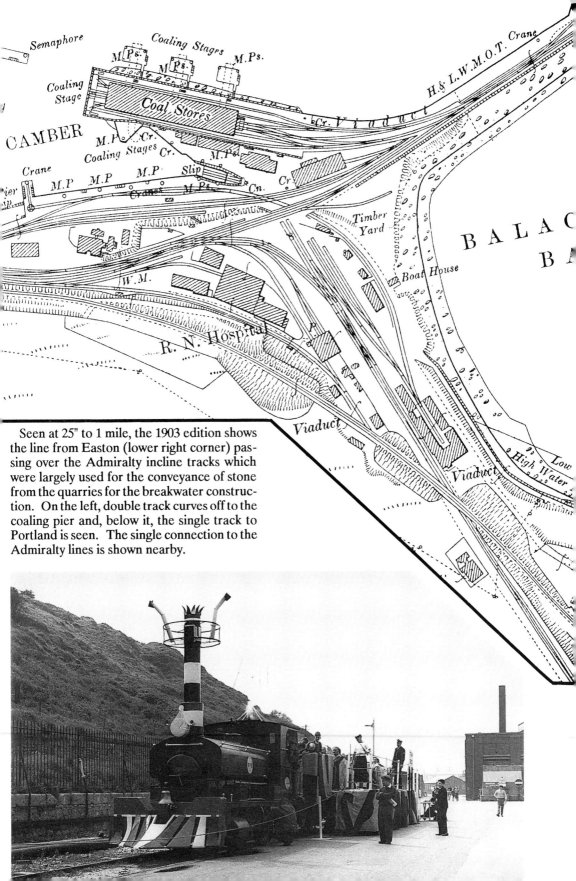

Semaphore

Coaling Stages   M.Ps.
M.Ps.
M.Ps.
Coaling   H.& L.W.M.O.T. Crane
Stage
Coal Stores   Cr. Viaduct
CAMBER   M.P   Cr.
Coaling Stages   Cr.   M.Ps.
Crane   M.P.   Slip   Cr.
Pier   M.P   M.P   M.P   M.Ps.   Cn.   Cr.
Slip   Cranes
Timber
Yard
BALAC
B
W.M.   Boat House
R. N. Hospital
Viaduct
High Water   Low
Viaduct
Viaduct   High Water

Seen at 25" to 1 mile, the 1903 edition shows
the line from Easton (lower right corner) passing over the Admiralty incline tracks which
were largely used for the conveyance of stone
from the quarries for the breakwater construction. On the left, double track curves off to the
coaling pier and, below it, the single track to
Portland is seen. The single connection to the
Admiralty lines is shown nearby.

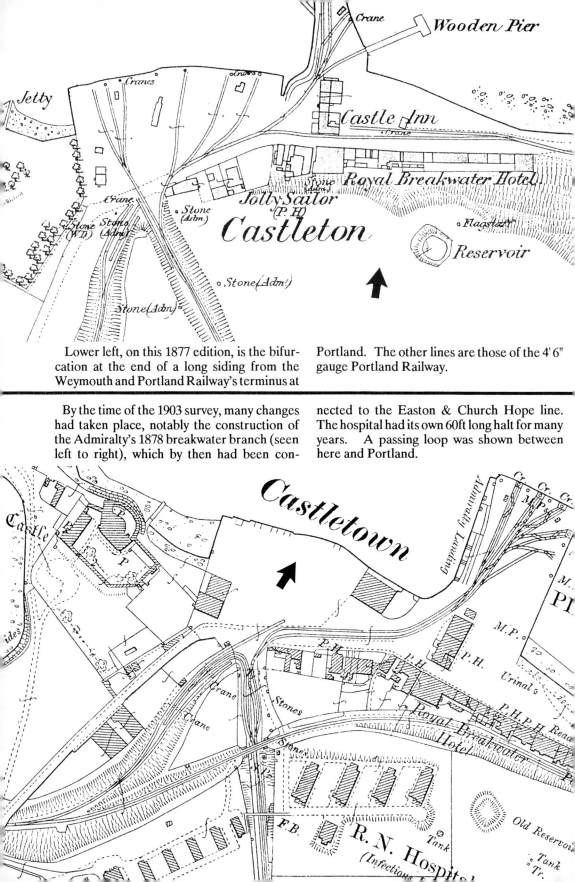

Lower left, on this 1877 edition, is the bifurcation at the end of a long siding from the Weymouth and Portland Railway's terminus at Portland. The other lines are those of the 4' 6" gauge Portland Railway.

By the time of the 1903 survey, many changes had taken place, notably the construction of the Admiralty's 1878 breakwater branch (seen left to right), which by then had been connected to the Easton & Church Hope line. The hospital had its own 60ft long halt for many years. A passing loop was shown between here and Portland.

PORTLAND

20. Services commenced on 16th October 1865, the terminus being situated close to the southern end of Chesil Beach. Although damaged, this print reveals the locomotives name to be *Nelson*. (R. C. Riley coll.)

21. The second station came into use in stages, the down platform being used from 2nd January 1905 and the up platform being available from 7th May 1905. Note the timber framework of the former, which was built on the foreshore. (Lens of Sutton)

22. A view south shows the limestone mass of the Isle of Portland, together with the steeply inclined streets of Fortuneswell. Right of centre is the goods shed, created from the terminal station, and to the right of that is F.J. Barnes' stone works. On the far left is the second station. (Lens of Sutton)

The map of 1877 illustrates the problems of a dual gauge railway. The siding to Castleton (top) is mixed gauge while two others are shown as broad gauge only. The shingle of Chesil Beach is at the bottom and the mud of Portland Harbour is at the top.

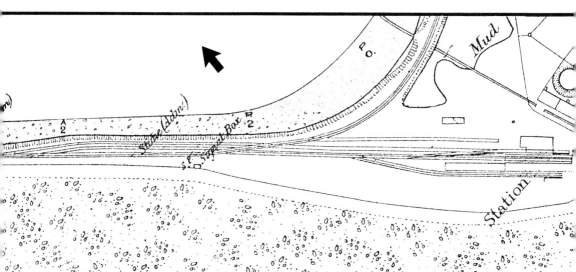

The 1903 edition reveals the exceptional number of cranes required for the stone traffic. At this time, trains between Easton and Weymouth had to reverse in or out of the station.

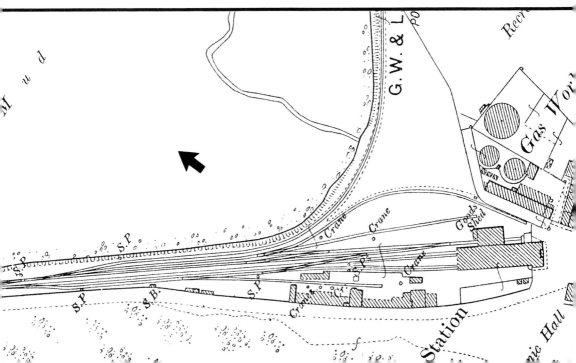

23. The fully enclosed footbridge must have been a blessing on many windy days - few trees tolerate the winds of Portland. Class O2 no. 207 runs into the down platform with an up train, presenting passengers with unexpected use of the footbridge. (Lens of Sutton)

24. Dereliction greeted participants of the Railway Enthusiasts Club railtour on 7th June 1958. The push-pull set started at Bournemouth West and visited Wimborne, Hamworthy, Upwey and West Bay. The two coaches were in the charge of class M7 no. 30107. (R. M. Casserley)

25. The east end of the station was recorded on the same day. A signal box was in use at the far end of the up platform, along with another near the junction with the goods yard, from 7th May 1905 until 22nd October 1935. They were replaced by a single box situated mid-way between the two. This was destroyed by enemy action in 1940 and replaced by one nearby. (R. M. Casserley)

26. The line closed when goods services were withdrawn on 5th April 1965. This northward view shows the original passenger platform in use for freight traffic and naval oil storage tanks in the distance. (Lens of Sutton)

27. Originally fitted with a small canopy, the terminal building served as a goods office for 60 years. Photographed in October 1965, it was eventually demolished to make way for the present roundabout. (J. H. Lucking)

28. Chesil Bank is over nine miles in length, running from Abbotsbury to Portland. No. 7780 is seen running over the southern end of it in 1956, heading towards Weymouth. Portland Harbour is on the left. (C. L. Caddy coll.)

29. Road access to the Isle of Portland was established in 1839, when the Ferry Bridge over the Fleet was completed. The railway crossing was known as Fleet Viaduct and is seen on 25th August 1963 as no. 4689 hauls a special train to Easton, with no. 7782 at the rear. (S. C. Nash)

30. Looking at the other side of the viaduct on 13th February 1965, we witness the passage of class 2 no. 41293, bound for Portland. In the background is Whitehead's Torpedo Works. (C. L. Caddy)

WYKE REGIS HALT

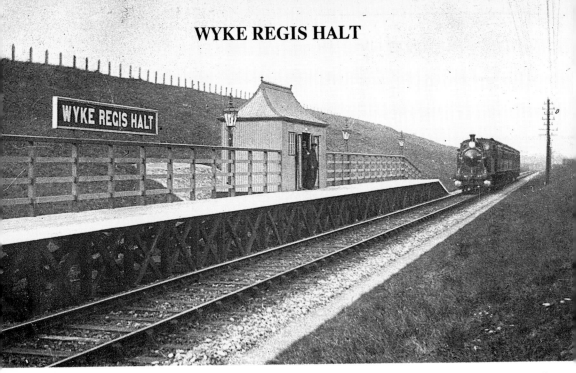

31. The halt was opened on 1st July 1909 and the platform was lengthened in February 1913. Access was by a lengthy footpath, shown on the map. (Lens of Sutton)

32. A Portland bound goods passes over the embankment near Sandsfoot Castle Halt on 21st September 1963. The platform, opened on 1st August 1932, was longer than that at Easton and was situated on the coast side of the line. (C. L. Caddy)

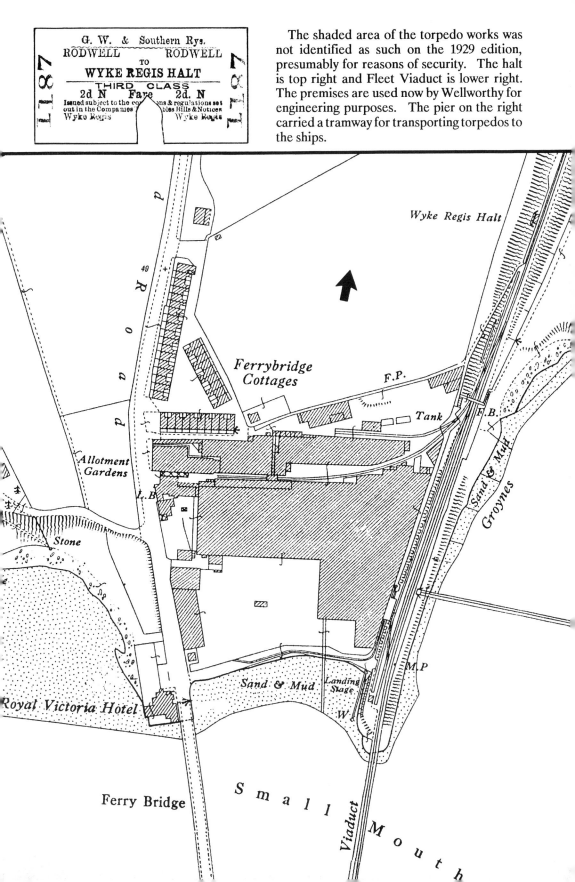

The shaded area of the torpedo works was not identified as such on the 1929 edition, presumably for reasons of security. The halt is top right and Fleet Viaduct is lower right. The premises are used now by Wellworthy for engineering purposes. The pier on the right carried a tramway for transporting torpedos to the ships.

Wyke Regis Halt

Ferrybridge
Cottages

F.P.

Tank

F.B.

Allotment
Gardens

L.B.

Sand & Mud

Groynes

Stone

M.P

Landing
Stage

W

Royal Victoria Hotel

Sand & Mud

Ferry Bridge

S m a l l

Viaduct

M o u t h

33. Half a mile north, another class 2 proceeds towards Portland on 6th February 1965 and passes under the bridge carrying Buxton Road, the A354. The trackbed is now occupied by a public nature path. (C. L. Caddy)

The 1929 edition indicates that access to the station was by way of an inclined footpath. The Poor Law buildings became part of Portwey Hospital, which was in use until 1986.

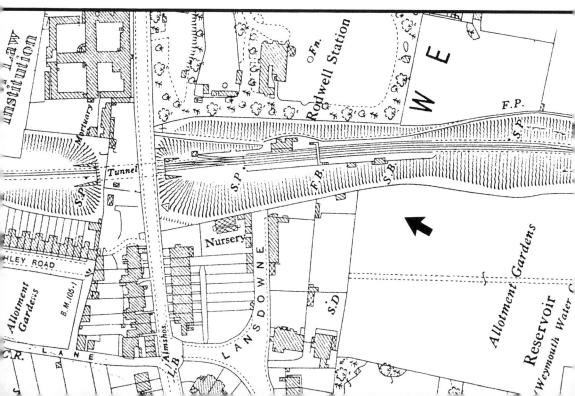

RODWELL

Rodwell Station Weymouth

34. The single platform, on the east side of the line, was opened in May 1870, to serve the developing residential area. The view is from Wyke Road. (Lens of Sutton)

35. The bulbous lady is standing on the tunnel carrying the wires to the small signal box, which was opened on 15th December 1892. No goods facilities were provided.
(Lens of Sutton)

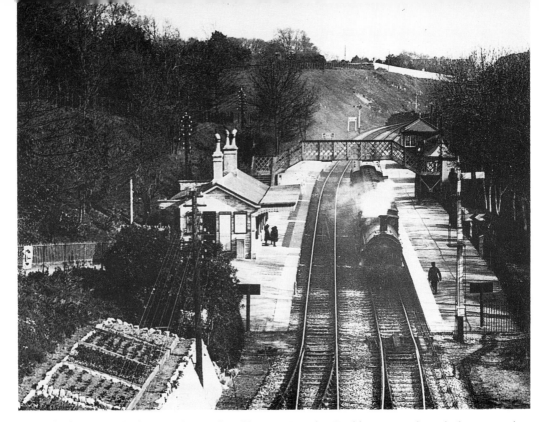

36. The loop, up platform and new signal box came into use on 8th December 1907, increasing the line capacity very considerably. The main buildings were enlarged substantially. (Lens of Sutton)

37. The 58yd long tunnel carried one running line and a short siding used by the engineeers. The footbridge dated from the 1907 alterations but the glasshouse was a private staff venture. (Lens of Sutton)

38. Viewed from above the tunnel on 24th July 1939, class O2 no. 185 restarts its up freight train, while sister O2 no. 177 leaves with the 4.00pm from Melcombe Regis.
(J. R. W. Kirkby)

39. The main buildings were destroyed and the signal box was damaged by bombs during WWII. Class M7 no. 30177 departs south with the 4.05pm from Melcombe Regis on 1st March 1952, the day that the station closed. (S. C. Nash)

40. The signal box and the loop remained in use until 1st March 1954, this March 1963 photograph showing that the track was retained much longer. The points were clipped and padlocked but could be used in an emergency. (C. L. Caddy)

41. Littlefield Crossing was adjacent to the halt (opened on 1st July 1909) access to which was by a path close to the fence on the left. A down train approaches the signal box, which contains a wheel for operating the gates. It remained functional until the end of goods services in 1965, the track being lifted in 1970. (Lens of Suton)

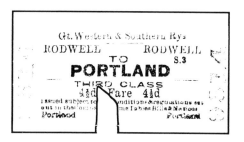

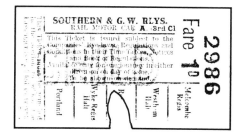

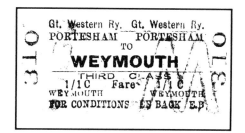

MELCOMBE REGIS

42. The station was built at the north end (right) of the viaduct over the Backwater, which once continued north to Radipole. This is the original timber structure which remained in use until 1909. (D. Cullum coll.)

43. The station was opened 44 years after the branch, on 30th May 1909, to reduce congestion and reversals at Weymouth station. It was named after the area in which it was situated, "Weymouth" originally describing the area south of the harbour. (Lens of Sutton)

44. The replacement all steel Backwater Viaduct was shorter than its predecessor, the reclaimed land being used for the new station. (Lens of Sutton)

45. The main line station is beyond the massive goods shed, on the right. Through passengers had a long walk after the opening of this station, but porterage was provided for luggage. The main feature is one of the GWR's 85O class. (Lens of Sutton)

46. Once bliss for lovers of birds and trains, further land reclamation has taken place and a busy roundabout now occupies the site. (Lens of Sutton)

47. Class O2 no. 189 bears the prefix E for Eastleigh, the SR using letters before renumbering their locomotive fleet by the addition of 1000 and 2000 to ex-SECR and ex-LBSCR engines. The guard is wearing a cash satchel for collection of fares at the halts. (Lens of Sutton)

48. A pair of O2s are viewed from the road that passed under the viaduct and ran along the shore of Radipole Lake. The class was built between 1889 and 1895 and most were still in use in the 1950s. (Lens of Sutton)

49. To retard an invading force, concrete tank traps were cast at strategic locations early in WWII. They were less easy to remove after the war, often being used for land reclamation. (Lens of Sutton)

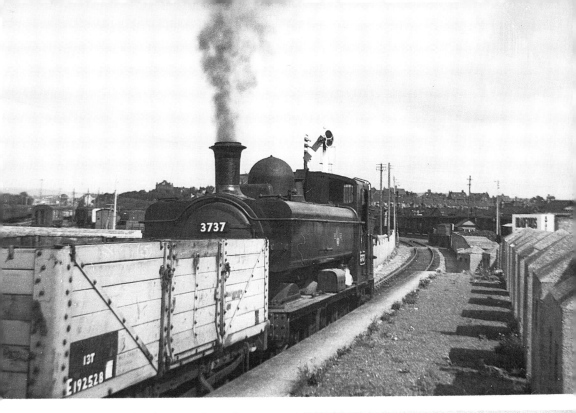

51. Freight from Portland passes through towards the junction in August 1960, the "Jubilee" sidings being in the left background. The platform continued to be used by passenger trains on summer Saturdays until 1959, to relieve pressure on the main terminal platforms. (C. L. Caddy coll.)

52. This public footpath notice was close to the northern limit of the Portland line and was photographed in 1948, with Weymouth goods shed in the background. (S. W. Baker)

← 50. The Railway Enthusiasts Club's train called at the station on 7th June 1958 to photograph it and its unusual wind shield. The lamps and windows retained their glass despite over six years of disuse. (R. M. Casserley)

PORTLAND JOINT RAILWAY
WARNING
DO NOT CROSS THE LINE WHILE THE BELL IS RINGING
BY ORDER

53. Postal packets to the Channel Islands began to operate regularly in 1794 and in 1889 the GWR took over the route; from that year passenger trains began to run to the pier, as seen here sometime between 1901 and 1907. (Lens of Sutton)

54. A slightly later view shows that The Pavilion of holiday Weymouth rubs shoulders with the Quay of commercial Weymouth near the end of the line. The headland on the right which gives protection to the harbour is The Nothe, a corruption of The Nose. (Lens of Sutton)

55. Five coaches project beyond the platform, a common problem resolved with short flights of five steps leant against the running board. Long trains were split to allow passengers to walk between the coaches, which were always those of the GWR until 1948. (Lens of Sutton)

56. The pier was reconstructed in 1931-33 and two tracks with two platforms were provided. These were increased to three following further redevelopment in 1961, the result being photographed in 1962. "4" refers to the speed limit for road vehicles. (C. L. Caddy)

57. Despite improvements, the small area of the site resulted in congestion, particularly severe during import of tomatoes and broccoli from the Channel Islands and during the holiday season. Ex-GWR 0-6-0T no. 1368 is shunting on 21st September 1956. (T. Wright)

58. The limited clearances are evident when viewed from an arriving boat train on 13th July 1960. No. 1368 waits to leave with a van train, while an Austin 10 stands close to the reconstruction work. Goods traffic ceased on 28th February 1972 as there was insufficient space in which to handle the developing container traffic. (H. C. Casserley)

59. No. 1369 was a tram engine from March 1960 until June 1962 and is now resident on the Dart Valley Railway at Buckfastleigh. Note the obligatory bell by the toolbox. The larger pannier tank is no. 4624 and is carrying a warning board normally put on the rear of a train of loose coupled wagons. Upon stopping, these trains were likely to rebound into motorists who came too close behind. (C. L. Caddy)

60. Photographed on 12th August 1972 is the new Quay building, one of the Drewry 240hp diesel shunters in platform 3 and oil tank wagons in platform 2. The oil was for bunkering the ships and was usually delivered twice a week in the summer until September 1983. (E. Wilmshurst)

61.   The trial run of a DMU is seen on 3rd March 1983, prior to the operation of a regular Bristol service during the following two summers.   Owing to the absence of a bell, a shunter was required to carry one ahead of the train, giving the appearance of the town crier. The original baggage hall was still standing in 1989.   (C. L. Caddy)

QUAY TRAMWAY

63. Three views from Town Bridge show the conflict between the railway, other road users, fishermen and those wishing to park their cars. An LCGB railtour proceeds towards the Quay on 3rd July 1966, hauled by 2-6-2T no. 41298. During WWII, a train ferry terminal was built to the right of this picture, but it was never used. (J. Scrace)

2nd - SINGLE	SINGLE - 2nd
(5966A) (07 Set 2)	(07 Set 2) (5966A)
Weymouth Quay to	
Weymouth Quay	Weymouth Quay
Bournemouth	Bournemouth
BOURNEMOUTH	
(S)	(S)
For conditions see over	For conditions see over

0247 ... 0247

62. Scheduled services ceased on 26th September 1987 and a number of special trains were operated that year, such as this Hastings line DEMU on its swansong on 8th August. Platform 3 had been abandoned in 1973 and the track shortened for use as a fuel oil siding. (R. E. Ruffell)

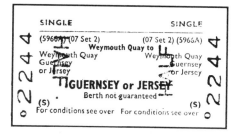

SINGLE	SINGLE
(5966A) (07 Set 2)	(07 Set 2) (5966A)
Weymouth Quay to	
Weymouth Quay	Weymouth Quay
Guernsey	Guernsey
or Jersey	or Jersey
GUERNSEY or JERSEY	
Berth not guaranteed	
(S)	(S)
For conditions see over	For conditions see over

0244 ... 0244

64. An up boat train on 12th August 1972 is composed of Mk. I coaches and diesel no. 2197. This class of locomotive operated on the tramway between 1962 and 1972. Farthings siding had been situated on the left until 1939. (E. Wilmshurst)

Top right

65. Class 33s began to be used regularly on the tramway in May 1973, no. 33110 being seen here on 23rd May 1981 with the 15.30 up boat train. Two cars had to be moved from its path, causing considerable delay. (J. Petley)

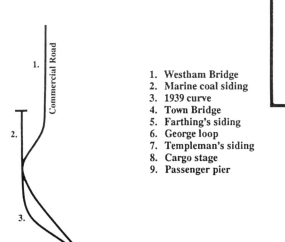

1. Westham Bridge
2. Marine coal siding
3. 1939 curve
4. Town Bridge
5. Farthing's siding
6. George loop
7. Templeman's siding
8. Cargo stage
9. Passenger pier

Diagram to show the optimum layout at the pier and the position of some of the earlier sidings.

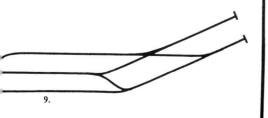

9.

66. The present Town Bridge dates from 1930 and is viewed from the "Hastings Diesel Swansong" on 8th August 1987. Flooding at high tide in bygone days had been known to extinguish the fire of locomotives with bad fitting dampers.
(R. E. Ruffell)

67. The left hand arch behind the Humber Super Snipe had once accommodated the tramway. The line was transferred from it to the right arch in 1938. No. 1369 proceeds about its business in August 1961. (T. Wright)

68. A class 12 0-6-0 diesel approaches Ferry's Corner, where the line turns from west to north. This class was to be seen on the tramway between 1967 and 1968. The flagman walks ahead in July 1967 to comply with the 1880 requirements. The majority prefer to look at the boats. (J. H. Bird)

69. Running in the reverse direction on the same day is no. D2043. In earlier days, special long link couplings had to be put on and corridor gangways had to be disconnected before reaching this curve, but track realignments in 1939 made this unnecessary. (J. H. Bird)

←

70. The Quay was widened north of Ferry's Corner by the GWR in 1938-39, permitting a larger radius curve to be laid. The old route was retained as a loop and is seen in the foreground of this 1961 photograph. Points were worked with a removable lever and there was no block system, pilot working being permitted. (T. Wright)

←

71. No. 73134 *Woking Homes 1885-1985* heads the Woking Homes railtour on 21st May 1988, with no. 33112 at the other end of the train of 4TC sets. It grinds against the check rail, accompanied by flagmen and cameramen. The last special in 1988 ran on 5th December. (J. H. Bird)

72. The six different members of the 1366 class worked on the tramway, collectively covering the period 1935 to 1962. One of them proceeds along Commercial Road to the Quay in August 1961, with the New Bridge Inn in the background. (T. Wright)

73. Road traffic had increased markedly by the next decade and more delays ensued. This van driver took some time to locate and British Transport Police have limited authority on the public highway. (C. Hall)

74. No. D2398 passes the road junction at the end of Westham (or New) Bridge with the 15.50 from the Quay on 7th July 1971. In front of the radiator is a detachable bell and flashing beacon unit and to the right of it are the high level hoses added for use with 4TC coaches. (J. Scrace)

75. The Hertfordshire Railtours' "Pines Pullman" proceeds towards the Quay on 29th June 1985, hauled by no. 33008 *Eastleigh* . When the tramway opened, the long straight Commercial Road was on the shore line.
(C. L. Caddy)

76. Due to a shortage of class 33s, the up boat train on the morning of 16th June 1984 was hauled by electro-diesels. Two were required (nos. 73125 and 73138) as they have limited power when running on diesel.
(B. L. Jackson)

77. At Weymouth Junction, the tramway engine was attached to down boat trains. No. 1367 is moving forward, the rear of the main line locomotive (just detached) is to the left of it. The other Pannier tank is standing in a siding, the route to the Quay passing in front of the houses in the distance. The Portland line is on the right of this July 1960 photograph. (H. C. Casserley)

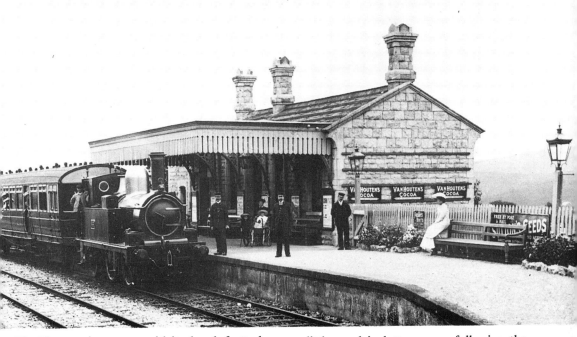

78. The massive canopy with its deeply fretted valance extended a wide welcome over passengers arriving at this charming country terminus, built of warm yellowish stone. The loop was little used in latter years, following the introduction of push-pull working with autocoaches. (Lens of Sutton)

79. A view from the west includes a typical GWR autocoach and a van standing at the cattle dock, behind the nameboard. The village of about 600 inhabitants has many attractive old buildings, including a 14th century barn. (Lens of Sutton)

80. Visitors have come to Abbotsbury for generations to see the swannery established in the 14th century at the western end of The Fleet and usually comprising about 500 birds. The sub-tropical gardens were and still are another attraction. The smoke is coming from a steam railmotor and cattle trucks are visible on the right. (E. H. Seward/Lens of Sutton)

81. Like Portesham, the village nestles at the foot of chalk downland, seen rising on the left. The station stood isolated, a quarter of a mile west of habitation, the approach diverging from the road to Portesham.
(E. H. Seward/Lens of Sutton)

82. Peace reigns as the empty autocoach waits for a passenger, a clerestory coach reflecting in its windows. A van stands outside the typical GWR goods shed which was still standing in 1989. A 30cwt crane was provided.
(Lens of Sutton)

83. Pictured not long before closure, the elegant lamps had given way to one under the reduced canopy. When opened, the terminus had a 16 x 48ft engine shed beyond the goods shed, with a 40 x 12ft coal stage. By 1896, the turntable was described as "buried". (C. L. Caddy coll.)

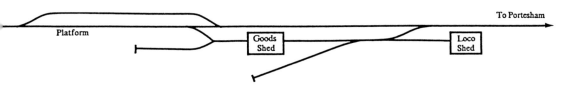

To Portesham

Platform

Goods Shed

Loco Shed

PORTESHAM

84. The small station was situated south west of the village of about 500 people, close to the Weymouth road. The 15th century church and the chalk mass of Portesham Hill are in the background.
(E. H. Seward/J. H. Lucking coll.)

85. A westward view includes the 30cwt crane, a camping coach and well tended gardens. In the early years of the century, a goods loop extended east to a quarry and a signal box stood to the left of the camera position. (Lens of Sutton)

86. The severe weather of February 1963 isolated numerous Dorset villages and many wished that the railway was still open. The loading gauge stood like gallows in the biting east wind which kept temperatures below freezing for over three months. The building now serves as a private dwelling. (C. L. Caddy)

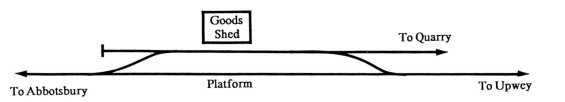

Goods
Shed

To Quarry

Platform

To Abbotsbury

To Upwey

UPWEY

87. To the right of the goods shed is the signal box which was in use until 1904. In the foreground is one of two ground frames that replaced it. (Lens of Sutton)

89. In common with th other branch stations, t canopy was cut back and camping coach was pr vided. The goods ya crane differed howeve being of a 6-ton capacity. (Lens of Sutton)

88. Like the other two stations on the branch, the station was on the south side of the line and was of similar design. Although one mile from Upwey, it was close to the village of Broadway, after which it was named until 1913, the suffix "Dorset" being added in 1906.
(E. H. Seward/Lens of Sutton)

90. The entire branch closed on 1st December 1952, except that freight facilities were retained here until 1st January 1962. This July 1961 photograph shows the new ballast and concrete sleepers which were removed in 1965. The building is now incorporated into industrial premises. (R. M. Casserley)

The 1929 map indicates two signal boxes which in fact only housed ground frames. The millstream passes under the goods yard.

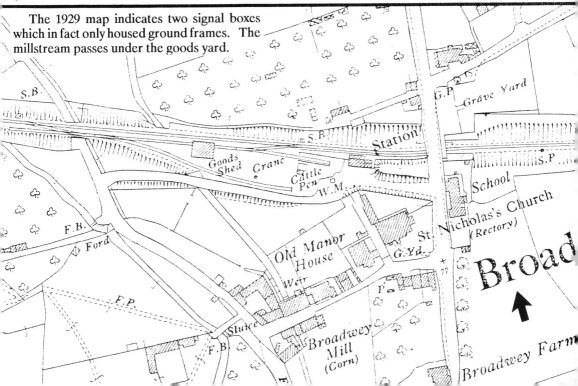

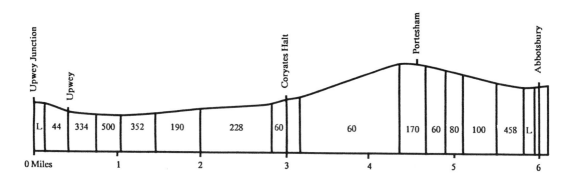

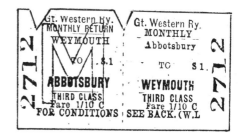

91. This junction station was opened on 19th April 1886 and superseded the original platforms for Upwey, which were to the north. The southward view from the footbridge shows the branch joining the up main line.
(Lens of Sutton)

92.　Looking north, we see that the branch platform was at a lower level than the up one. The main part of Upwey village is in the distance.　The gold cup, used by King George III to drink from the wishing well there, later gained fame at Ascot Races. (Lens of Sutton)

93.　Photographed against the sun, 0-4-2T no. 1467 propels its autocoach from the branch towards the junction crossover, to gain the down line to Weymouth.　(C. L. Caddy coll.)

94. A northward panorama in 1961 includes the eleven and a half chain curve, which descended at 1 in 44 towards Abbotsbury. The original Upwey station was close to the houses in the background. (H. C. Casserley)

96. Western Region DMUs provided most of the services to Upwey until electrification in May 1988 gave the station an hourly service to Waterloo throughout the day. The 10.24 Swindon to Weymouth train stops over the recently laid conductor rail on 16th March 1988. (J. Scrace)

95. Most of the branch was lifted in 1955, only the points remaining on 6th September 1966. They are visible behind the rear coach of the 16.47 Weymouth to Bournemouth Central. The signal box remained in use until 1st March 1970. (J. Scrace)

97. The timber built halt was opened on 1st July 1905 to serve the northern suburbs of Weymouth, which were developing at that time. No. 4803 is running northwards, probably destined for Abbotsbury. The last train called on 31st December 1983.
(Lens of Sutton)

BRITISH RAILWAYS (S)
This ticket is issued subject to the Bye-laws, Regulations and Conditions contained in the Publications and Notices of and applicable to the Railway Executive.
Upwey Junction to
Upwey Junction   Upwey Junction
Radipole Halt   Radipole Halt
RADIPOLE HALT
THIRD CLASS   THIRD CLASS
Fare 3½d.   Fare 3½d.
NOT TRANSFERABLE
3126

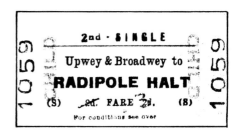

2nd · SINGLE
Upwey & Broadway to
RADIPOLE HALT
(S)   FARE   (B)
For conditions see over
1059

98. *Cwm Mawr* was on the allocation on 16th June 1935, having been inherited by the GWR when it incorporated the Burry Port & Gwendraeth Valley Railway in 1923. Note the tramway bell by the injector. The coal stage had been built in 1930. (S. W. Baker)

The 1890 survey indicates the tide line. Land reclamation resulted in three sidings and a road being built on the foreshore. Radipole Lake is now freshwater and is noted for appearances of the rare Bearded Tit. Twelve additional sidings were laid later on the eastern part of the depot.

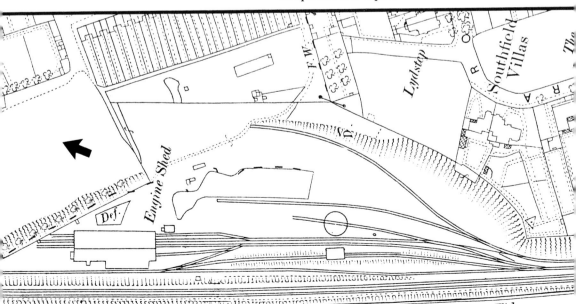

99. The main line rises at 1 in 187 in the background and one of the three "Jersey" sidings is seen beyond. This 1961 view from the north end of the shed roof features the enginemen's lobby and part of the fleet of 17 locomotives, coaled up ready for traffic. (C. Attwell)

100. From the same vantage point, the 60ft turntable can be seen. It replaced the 45ft diameter one, shown on the map, in 1930. The crane had been used for clearing a massive stockpile of coal that had earlier stretched across the tracks. (C. Attwell)

101. Class 2 no. 41261 and "West Country" no. 34013 *Okehampton* are visible, as is the winding drum of the locomotive hoist. Attached to it is a small hoist on a jib, which was used for lifting heavy engine parts, such as connecting rods. The date is 3rd February 1965. (R. E. Ruffell)

102. The GWR did not favour the tall mechanical coaling systems used on other railways, owing to the friable nature of the Welsh coal commonly used. No. 35012 *United States Lines* stands amid the ash heaps on 11th February 1967. Lack of labour resulted in a tractor shovel being hired periodically to clear the yard. (E. Wilmshurst)

103. The three road shed was built in 1885 and superseded a small one situated nearer to the station. Class 4 2-6-0 no. 76006 is under the gantry on 28th May 1967, its rear driving wheels having been rolled out. (T. Wright)

104. Weymouth was the terminus of the last steam worked main line from London. The shed closed when steam ceased on 9th July 1967 and, by the end of May, the yard was clogged with withdrawn locomotives. From left to right are no. 73002, 35014 and 35026. All the track was lifted in 1970 and dwellings now occupy the site. (T. Wright)

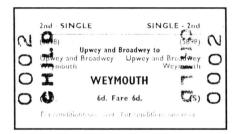

2nd · SINGLE   SINGLE · 2nd
(5898)   (5898)
Upwey and Broadwey to
Upwey and Broadwey   Upwey and Broadwey
Weymouth   Weymouth
WEYMOUTH
6d. Fare 6d.   (S)
For conditions see over   For conditions see over

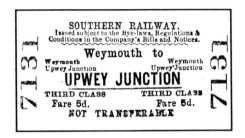

SOUTHERN RAILWAY.
Issued subject to the Bye-laws, Regulations &
Conditions in the Company's Bills and Notices.
Weymouth to
Weymouth   Weymouth
Upwey Junction   Upwey Junction
UPWEY JUNCTION
THIRD CLASS   THIRD CLASS
Fare 5d.   Fare 5d.
NOT TRANSFERABLE

WEYMOUTH

The 1864 survey shows numerous wagon turntables, the position of the original goods shed and two locomotive sheds, GWR extreme left and LSWR near the centre.

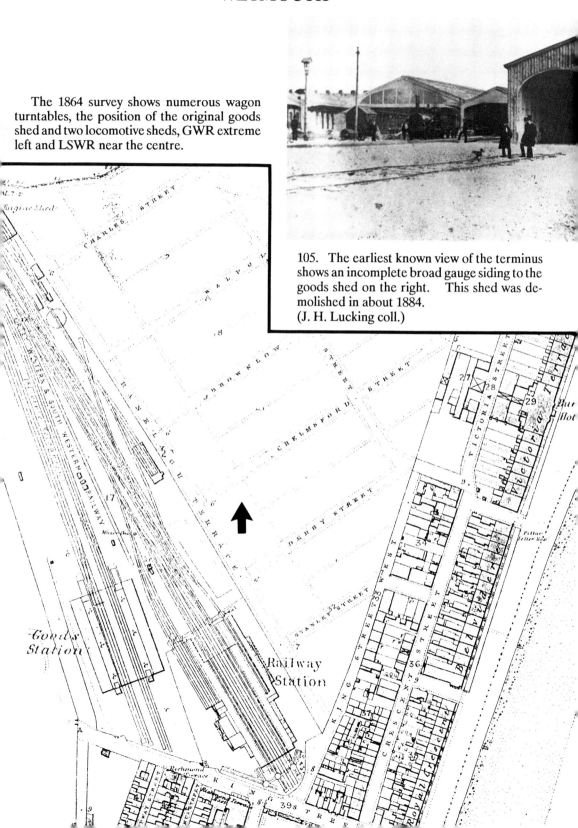

105. The earliest known view of the terminus shows an incomplete broad gauge siding to the goods shed on the right.   This shed was demolished in about 1884.
(J. H. Lucking coll.)

106. Station Box is at the end of the platform and the roof of Junction Box is visible to the left of it. On the right is the water tank on columns, the adjacent LSWR locomotive shed being obscured by stock. (Lens of Sutton)

The 1902 map includes the LSWR engine shed, which remained in use until January 1939, after which the Portland branch engines were transferred to the GWR depot. Melcombe Regis station was opened in 1909, close to the word "Viaduct", but was built on newly reclaimed land. The single line of the Quay Tramway is shown running to the lower right corner of the map, and the Esplanade, so popular with day visitors and holidaymakers, is at the top right. Junction Box is marked S. B. (half way across this page), while Station Box is to be found at the end of the longest platform.

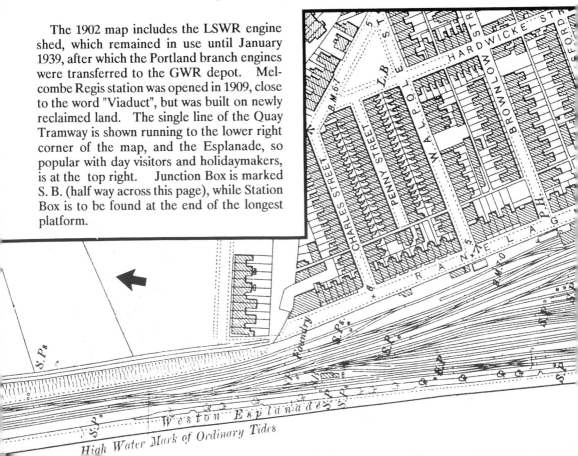

107. The population of the town trebled to 15,000 during the latter half of the last century and holiday traffic increased at a greater rate. The lack of platforms at the three centre roads was no doubt later regretted. The van is standing at a dock, unsuitable for holiday trains. A backing signal is nearby. (Lens of Sutton)

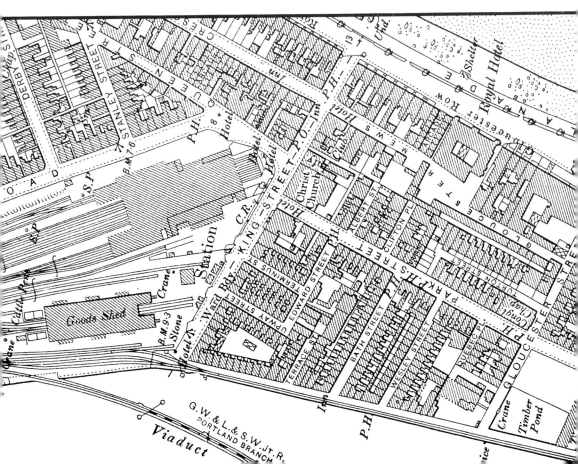

108. The overall roof was removed in 1951,
the glass having been taken out at the begin-
ning of WWII. This 1956 panorama includes

Radipole Lake on the left and land on the right
being prepared for the new platforms, which
remain in use today. (Weymouth Museum)

109.   The Brunel style building with its deep eaves was in poor condition when photographed in June 1963 in the company of Austin's latest competitor to the railway.   Note that the shapely canopy brackets were augmented by aerial stays.
(Lens of Sutton)

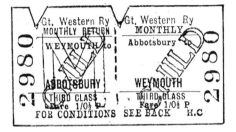

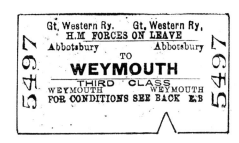

110. Class 5 4-6-0 no. 73118 *King Leodegrance* was far from steam tight on 29th May 1967 and was assisted by no. D7045. Up passengers were frequently banked up the four mile climb to Bincombe Tunnel, much of which was at 1 in 50. The ramps in the foreground were for the GWR system of automatic train control. (T. Wright)

111.   On the same day, Drewry diesel no. D2295 hauled empty stock from the platforms on the up main.   On the left is the double track for engine movements and those on the right were mainly for goods traffic.   The gable end of the goods shed is in the distance. (T. Wright)

112.   Many special trains and high speed runs were made in the last week of steam operation.   One of the former arrived on 7th May 1967, behind no. 34023 *Blackmore Vale* which is now resident on the Bluebell Railway.   The odd shape of the canopy resulted from the removal of the overall roof.   (R. E. Ruffell)

3306
BRITISH RAILWAYS (S)
This ticket is issued subject to the Bye-laws, Regulations and Conditions contained in the Publications and Notices of and applicable to the Railway Executive.
Cheap Day as advertised
Weymouth to
ABBOTSBURY
Third Class
NOT TRANSFERABLE
BRITISH RAILWAYS (S)
CHEAP DAY
Abbotsbury
Weymouth
Abbotsbury to
WEYMOUTH
Third Class
3306

113.   The injector leaks steam as worn-out class 5 no. 73085 waits to leave with the 10.17 stopping train to Bournemouth on 1st June 1967.   The two tracks into the massive goods shed were removed in 1973.   (T. Wright)

114. Steam was nearly at the end of the road when no. 34040 *Crewkerne*, devoid of its name-plate, was photographed at platform 4 on 29th May 1967. 28 Trailer Control sets (4TC) were built for diesel haulage or propulsion and no. 76279 illustrates the change to come. (T. Wright)

115. A travelling post office operated between Waterloo and Dorchester for decades and on 27th November 1961 it was extended to Weymouth. It ceased to operate in May 1988 and is seen in platform 5 which, with no. 6, came into use on 14th April 1957. (D. Clayton)

116. Another photograph from June 1971 shows an arrival from Waterloo, headed by no. D7014. The five sidings in the background were added in 1960 but were little used after 14th August 1972 when goods facilities were withdrawn. (D. Clayton)

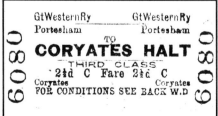

117. Junction Box and Station Box were both closed on 14th April 1957 and replaced by this one, seen in September 1978. It ceased to be manned on 19th September 1987, when operations were controlled from a panel at Dorchester South. (J. Scrace)

118. A Bristol service stands at the old platform 4 on 29th August 1979, as track lifting proceeds. The last remains of the old station were demolished in the Spring of 1986. (M. Turvey)

Other photographs and maps of the route from Upwey Junction to Weymouth appear in our *Bournemouth to Weymouth* album.

119. Two trains, each composed of two 4TC sets with class 33 diesels at the far end, stand in the 1957 platforms on 6th May 1985. The right hand train had started from Weymouth Quay and had reversed into the platform. (R. E. Ruffell)

120. Platforms 5 and 6 were renumbered 2 and 3 and a new number 1 was provided in July 1987, mainly for use by Western Region trains. When photographed on 2nd May 1988, shot blasting of the 1957 steelwork was in progress and the conductor rail had been energised ready for the start of Weymouth's best ever service to London. (C. L. Caddy)

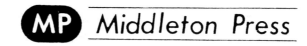

MP *Middleton Press*

Easebourne Lane, Midhurst, West Sussex, GU29 9AZ
Midhurst (0730) 813169

BRANCH LINES

BRANCH LINES TO MIDURST
BRANCH LINES AROUND MIDHURST
BRANCH LINES TO HORSHAM
BRANCH LINES TO ALTON
BRANCH LINE TO HAYLING
BRANCH LINE TO SOUTHWOLD
BRANCH LINE TO TENTERDEN
BRANCH LINES TO NEWPORT
BRANCH LINES TO TUNBRIDGE WELLS
BRANCH LINE TO SWANAGE
BRANCH LINES TO LONGMOOR
BRANCH LINE TO LYME REGIS
BRANCH LINE TO FAIRFORD
BRANCH LINE TO ALLHALLOWS
BRANCH LINES AROUND ASCOT
BRANCH LINES AROUND WEYMOUTH

SOUTH COAST RAILWAYS

BRIGHTON TO WORTHING
CHICHESTER TO PORTSMOUTH
BRIGHTON TO EASTBOURNE
RYDE TO VENTNOR
EASTBOURNE TO HASTINGS
PORTSMOUTH TO SOUTHAMPTON
SOUTHAMPTON TO BOURNEMOUTH
ASHFORD TO DOVER
BOURNEMOUTH TO WEYMOUTH

SOUTHERN MAIN LINES

WOKING TO PORTSMOUTH
HAYWARDS HEATH TO SEAFORD
EPSOM TO HORSHAM
CRAWLEY TO LITTLEHAMPTON
THREE BRIDGES TO BRIGHTON
WATERLOO TO WOKING
VICTORIA TO EAST CROYDON
TONBRIDGE TO HASTINGS
EAST CROYDON TO THREE BRIDGES
WOKING TO SOUTHAMPTON
WATERLOO TO WINDSOR
LONDON BRIDGE TO EAST CROYDON

COUNTRY RAILWAY ROUTES

BOURNEMOUTH TO EVERCREECH JUNCTION
READING TO GUILDFORD
WOKING TO ALTON
BATH TO EVERCREECH JUNCTION
GUILDFORD TO REDHILL
EAST KENT LIGHT RAILWAY

STEAMING THROUGH

STEAMING THROUGH KENT
STEAMING THROUGH EAST HANTS
STEAMING THROUGH SURREY
STEAMING THROUGH WEST SUSSEX
STEAMING THROUGH THE ISLE OF WIGHT
STEAMING THROUGH WEST HANTS

OTHER RAILWAY BOOKS

WAR ON THE LINE
GARRAWAY FATHER & SON
LONDON CHATHAM & DOVER RAILWAY
INDUSTRIAL RAILWAYS OF THE SOUTH EAST

OTHER BOOKS

MIDHURST TOWN THEN & NOW
EAST GRINSTEAD THEN & NOW

MILITARY DEFENCE OF WEST SUSSEX
SUSSEX POLICE FORCES

WEST SUSSEX WATERWAYS
SURREY WATERWAYS